ALLEN PHOTOGR

CW00891097

PREPARING FOR A DRESSAGE TEST

CONTENTS

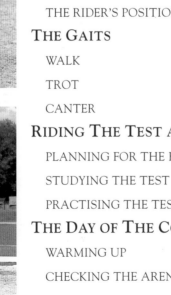

WHAT THE JUDGE EXPECTS TO SEE

Nothing of value is achieved unless the competitor identifies goals. He should picture his goal and train the horse gradually towards it. By following this strategy he converts nebulous ideas into concrete realities; then he can become a good dressage competitor.

The comments made on the test sheets give knowledge and direction. Understanding the judge's perspective adds effectiveness to competing so, consequently, this book illustrates what the judge expects to see at Preliminary, Novice and Elementary dressage competitions.

Here we see, at Preliminary level, free walk on a long rein (*right*). The Elementary horse shows a more advanced way of going; he is in collected trot (*below*).

Dressage competitions prove correctness of the training and measure the horse's balance and the rider's ability to tune into that balance. Used constructively, they motivate horse and rider.

The rider should appreciate that the judge wants to reward the horse with good marks wherever he can. He must possess the integrity to be fair to every competitor and he must have the knowledge to place them in the correct order of merit. To do this he awards marks from 0–10 for each test move-ment and for each

section of the collective marks: these are the general impressions of the gaits, impulsion, submission and the effects of the rider. Normally, the judge justifies each mark with a comment.

The judge expects to see: rhythm (a), acceptance of the bridle (b), impulsion (c), straightness (d), collection (e) and a correct, effective rider position (f), *see photos opposite*. These principles follow the scales of training and are expressed as follows: 1. three correct gaits; 2. the horse moving freely forwards with activity and

impulsion; 3. the horse being willing to accept the bridle and show suppleness and ease of the movements and, 4. the rider sitting in balance with the horse and riding with effective but unobtrusive aids.

RHYTHM

The three dressage gaits of walk, trot and canter should show regularity and be in the correct sequence of footfalls. Good rhythm is enhanced when the above criteria are united with energy and spring. This mare (*right*) is showing good rhythm in the working trot.

SUPPLENESS

The dressage horse must be supple laterally and longitudinally. Lateral suppleness relates to the body bend of the horse to the left and right. To remain straight when the horse is moving on turns and circles, for example, he contracts the muscles on the inside of his body and stretches the muscles on the outside. Ideally he should be equally supple on both reins.

Longitudinal suppleness relates to the suppleness of the horse's back from the poll to the tail (this is known as the top line). A supple horse uses his back muscles to round the back so that the energy can move through his body and he can step actively forwards to the bridle. This allows the rider to absorb the horse's movement and ride in harmony with the horse.

SUBMISSION (acceptance of the aids)

Submission covers many aspects of the horse's way of going and results in the horse accepting the aids with ease and readiness. When the horse accepts the bit with good submission, (i.e. he does not resist in his body or mind) and when he responds to the forward aids with impulsion (i.e. his hind-quarters are engaged so that the energy he creates can move through his back, withers, shoulders, neck, and poll to his jaw) he can move with *increasingly better degrees of submission*. These factors create a cycle of positive improvement and this, in turn, fine-tunes self-carriage.

To promote good submission the rider must not seek contact with the horse's mouth by pulling at the reins. It checks impulsion and compromises the gymnastic development of the horse. When the horse is encouraged by the rider to seek the bit he is physically able to engage his hindquarters, and with good training this will result in impulsion and submission. These two forces are intrinsically linked.

DAVID'S TIP

Familiarise yourself with the sequence of footfalls for the three gaits. You will find them explained on pages 11, 13 and 16.

Horses running free can be exuberant and show off by dancing with 'spring' in their steps. Dressage aims to emulate this, but it can only be achieved through correct, consistent dressage training. The degree to which spring can be improved depends on the talent of each horse.

There are examples of good submission throughout the book. These photos show *bad* examples; this mare is: above the bit and not 'round' through the back (a); overbent with too much inside bend (b); hollow in trot (c); very above the bit and being naughty (d).

DAVID'S TIP

As an approximate guide to whether or not a horse is overbent, imagine a vertical line drawn straight from his poll to his nose to the ground; often referred to as 'the vertical'. This term is used when appraising the horse's acceptance of the bit. If the horse's head is carried behind the vertical, the poll is unlikely to be the highest point of his body, but provided he *works into the bridle* this cannot be classified as a fault because the horse is working actively forwards. However, if he is behind the vertical and not working into the bridle, he is overbent and this is a serious fault.

Flexion The horse flexes his head at the poll with vertical and lateral flexion. With vertical flexion he flexes so that his nose is the lowest, and his poll the highest, point. When the horse can flex at the poll in either direction at the rider's request, without altering the line of travel through his body, lateral flexion is achieved. It is also known as inside bend and in tests the amount shown is small, i.e. approximately ½–1 in. Some movements require outside flexion, for example

counter canter, however the principle is the same except flexion is to the outside. (See *Riding a Dressage Test* for more details on counter canter.)

In dressage tests when the horse is asked to accept a contact with the bit he must show vertical and lateral flexion at the same time. The bay gelding pictured on this page shows lateral flexion.

DAVID'S TIP

When riding in an arena the terms 'inside' and 'outside' refer to the rein the horse is working on. If working on the left rein the inside is the left side and the outside is the right side.

The horse finds it easy to move his head vertically and laterally if there is room in his gullet to fit 2–3 fingers comfortably.

IMPULSION

This is controlled power created by the rider. Impulsion originates from engagement of the hindquarters and travels through the horse's body to an elastic contact. Suppling exercises such as turns, circles and lateral work, combined with transitions and half-halts convert energy into impulsion. It enhances the beauty of the horse's gaits.

This horse (*left*) demonstrates a balanced active trot and softness in the poll which indicates good acceptance of the rider's hands

DAVID'S TIP

Speed does not equal impulsion! Lots of small fast-moving strides indicate speed. With impulsion the horse moves actively forwards with rhythm and balance, whereas with speed he is running and out of rhythm. To develop good impulsion the horse must respond to the forward-asking aids generously and then he can move with big elevated strides. Sometimes the horse responds to the forward-asking aids well but, because of a lack of balance, the gaits quicken. The rider should keep the hands still and allow the horse to express his energy as impulsion.

The grey gelding below is not active with his hindquarters and is restricted in the neck.

STRAIGHTNESS

This mare shows good straightness for
Novice level dressage and shows good body
bend for a Novice horse.

The judge wants to see that the horse
moves straight, i.e. his hind legs must follow
in the same track as his front legs. The
horse should move straight on straight and
curved lines (this includes turns, corners
and circles). To remain straight on curved
lines the horse must *bend through his body*
and the amount of bend must correspond
to the curved line.

Body bend must be uniform throughout the length of the horse's body. If a horse is stiff to the left and working on a left circle, too much weight will fall on his inside shoulder and/or his hindquarters will move outside the line of the circle. If he works on a right circle, he will show too much inside body bend (ie curl up to the inside), carry his hindquarters inside the line of the circle and fall onto his outside shoulder. To be straight, the horse must be equally supple on both sides of his body.

The straightness required of a Novice horse is less demanding than that of a higher level dressage horse and test movements reflect this. For example, at Novice level the turns and figures are easier, the circles are larger whereas at Elementary level there are 10 m circles in trot and turns in collected canter. These movements demand higher levels of suppleness and straightness. This horse shows a lack of straightness (*right*).

COLLECTION

This becomes a test requirement from Elementary level onwards. Collection contains the horse's energy and gives elevation; the forehand lifts and the gaits become more expressive and beautiful. Collection is dependent on straightness, suppleness and impulsion.

THE RIDER'S POSITION

The horse is free to express the brilliance of his gaits when the rider sits in balance with his movement. The rider position guidelines of elbow-wrist-hand and shoulder-hip-heel are good precedents to follow but must allow for the different physical proportions of each rider and each horse.

However, there is more to riding good dressage than this! 'Feel' is very important. It improves as the rider gains experience, he learns *when* and *how* to apply the aids correctly and the horse's *responses to the aids* are improved. Once refined, feel becomes so light that the rider's directions seem to begin in the mind of the horse; horse and rider move in true partnership.

DAVID'S TIP

There is nothing more pleasing for the judge than to see that picture of beauty: the horse and rider moving as one, in harmony.

Rider Position Guidelines

Elbow-wrist-hand A soft elastic feel establishes good contact with the horse's mouth and acceptance of the bit (a).

Shoulder-hip-heel This leg position allows the rider to give the most sensitive and effective leg aids (b).

Sitting 'live' This means going with the horse's movement and not blocking his energy. This seat permits the horse to move to the maximum of his ability (c).

A straight back influences the weight distribution on the rider's seatbones which in turn can influence the horse's balance and suppleness (d).

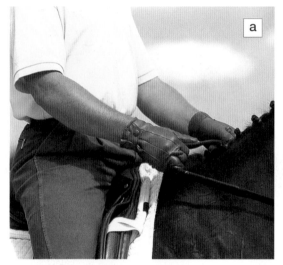

THE GAITS

WALK

Medium walk This is the natural walk of the horse. He marches forwards, generally overtracking and he accepts the bit with a soft steady contact. This mare (*right*) is showing a good medium walk.

Free walk on a long rein The horse is asked to march forwards in front of the rider's seat, is allowed to draw his head and neck down and forwards towards the ground with his nose slightly in front of the vertical and to move with his back and neck rounded. This allows maximum opportunity for relaxation and a chance to show a clear overtracking of the footfalls without losing the four-time rhythm. The

SEQUENCE OF FOOTFALLS

The horse marches forwards in a four-time rhythm so that four individual hoof beats can be heard: **1.** right hind foot, **2.** right fore foot, **3.** left hind foot, **4.** left fore foot. He has two or three feet on the ground at the same time. In the walk there is no moment of suspension. Each leg must move forward in the same regular rhythm and the same length of stride.

mare pictured below is demonstrating a lovely free walk with good overtracking and stretching of the head and neck.

DAVID'S TIP

The horse shows 'throughness', or is 'through', when the energy moves through his body in good coordination; then he maximises impulsion, rhythm and the brilliance of his gaits. When the horse is 'through' contact improves, the rider can communicate with the horse better. He can direct impulsion to the best advantage.

Extended walk (Elementary) At Elementary level the horse will be introduced to extended walk by being ridden forwards in a walk similar in activity to that displayed in free walk. The rider allows the horse to stretch his head and neck forward (keeping the contact) until the top line of the neck is approximately parallel with the ground. The walk strides cover as much ground as possible, but the activity should be without haste, and the regularity of the footfalls must be preserved in the four-beat rhythm of the walk.

TROT

Working trot This is the horse's natural trot with a touch more energy. All horses should track-up in the working trot and some overtrack. This depends on each horse's movement and conformation. For example, a horse with a long back may track-up, but not overtrack, in his working trot. The main criteria is that the working trot swings through in active, rhythmical steps and the horse remains in balance.

The horse steps in the working trot with good spring and in a regular rhythm. For the horse to show good diagonalisation the trot must be regular in rhythm and each diagonal step must match in length and expression.

SEQUENCE OF FOOTFALLS

The trot is a two-time movement with the legs moving in diagonal pairs. Listen to the horse moving in trot and you will hear two hoof beats. First beat: left diagonal (right hind leg and left foreleg); moment of suspension; second beat: right diagonal (left hind leg and right foreleg). When the left diagonal pair of legs is suspended, shortly before it is placed on the ground again the right diagonal pair has also been lifted; the horse is moving with all four legs in the air for a moment: this is the moment of suspension. The trot is regular in rhythm if the period of time each diagonal pair is lifted is the same.

Lengthened trot strides The horse moves with more engagement than in the working trot and responds by striding forwards into equally lengthened strides. Normally, he comes into the bridle more positively and the rider allows the hand to follow the contact in an elastic way. Ideally, the horse's head is slightly in front of the vertical and his neck is less arched than in the working trot. In the lengthened trot the horse shows clear overtracking.

To show equal movement, the angle of the forearm to the ground should match the angle of the hind cannon bone to the ground.

The novice mare (*top*) is showing good lengthened trot strides.

This gelding (*right*) is flicking his toes and not working equally through from behind.

Good lengthened trot strides (*below*). The horse is now working equally with his back and front ends and in better balance than in the photograph above.

DAVID'S TIP

In lengthened trot, if a horse tends to carry his head too high and flattens his back, ride him in a rounder outline before the movement. This should help him move with strides which match in front and behind. (This also applies to medium and extended trot.)

Medium trot (Elementary) Medium trot is developed through the lengthened trot. The horse's strides cover more ground than the working or lengthened trot strides (*right, top*). Normally, he becomes more powerful by carrying his neck less arched than in the working trot and with his head slightly in front of the vertical.

Once the collected trot and self-carriage of the horse develop, the lengthened trot strides become more powerful and, gradually through this increased balance, the medium trot improves.

> **DAVID'S TIP**
>
> From Elementary level upwards, medium trot should be ridden from marker to marker. In Novice tests the judge prefers to see a handful of balanced lengthened trot strides rather than unbalanced strides across the whole diagonal.

Collected trot (Elementary) Collected trot shows more elevation than the working trot. The strides show more spring from the contained energy of the collection, the hindquarters are more engaged and the head and neck carried higher. *In collection the horse must always be active and taking himself forwards.* Here the horse is slightly behind the vertical (*see above*).

> **DAVID'S TIP**
>
> The length of stride in the gaits is not the only measure of their correctness. The judge looks at other factors, i.e. balance, self-carriage and the ease with which the horse performs. As a guide, the horse should track-up in collected trot, overtrack in working trot and show a clear overtrack in medium trot.
>
> The amount of collection required at Elementary-level dressage is less than that expected in the higher level tests.

CANTER

Working canter This is the horse's natural canter with a touch more energy and with him working through to the bit.

In Preliminary tests, working canter is the only canter required. It is also the main canter at Novice level. Lengthened canter strides are introduced in a few Novice tests and continued at Elementary level. Although working canter still plays the primary role, collected canter is introduced in Elementary tests.

The top photo shows a good working canter with good self-carriage.

These horses, *see right and below*, display some faults in the canter: in photograph (a) she lacks engagement and is above the bit; in photograph (b) he is on the forehand.

SEQUENCE OF FOOTFALLS

If you listen to the horse moving in canter, you will hear three beats. If the horse is cantering on his left lead he moves forward in this way: first beat – right hind leg; second beat – left hind leg and right foreleg together; third beat – left foreleg; moment of suspension.

Lengthened canter strides When the working canter has improved in balance and forwardness and the horse has become straighter in this gait, the rider can begin to lengthen the canter strides.

At first, lengthening is shown on the long side of the arena because, if the horse is ridden intelligently prior to the lengthening, the canter can be straightened and balanced ready for the movement. If the rider asks for a *very slight* canter shoulder-fore as the horse comes out of the corner, and just before the lengthened strides, it helps straighten the horse. It promotes elevation to the lengthened strides because the horse's inside hind leg steps more under his body thereby lowering his hindquarters. Riding it this way helps balance and engagement.

In Novice tests lengthened canter strides are introduced for a handful of strides along the long side of the arena. The horse should remain balanced in the transitions, should not fall on his forehand, or lose straightness, and maintain good canter rhythm.

The horse in the top photo demonstrates a good 'uphill' lengthened canter and good lift of the forearm.

Medium canter (Elementary) (*Centre photo.*) This is the gait between working canter and extended canter. The strides jump forwards more with energetic steps that remain true to the canter three-time rhythm. The horse remains on the bit and normally he carries his head slightly in front of the vertical.

Collected canter (Elementary) The horse shows more lift through the shoulder (this is the beginning of elevation created by collection) and the quarters become more active. The strides cover less ground than in the working canter (*see right*).

RIDING THE TEST AT HOME

PLANNING FOR THE BIG DAY

Be well prepared if you want to be successful in competition dressage. Many people, and horses, perform under par when put under pressure but the secret of success is to use that adrenaline buzz positively. To increase confidence, **select the right test** and train the horse to a higher level at home than that at which he competes. For example, at home this grey gelding (*see right*) works in the half pass (Medium-level movement) but he competes at Elementary level. All this preparation primes you to be a successful competitor, whether you compete to win, or for experience or for training guidance.

Getting things right at home prepares you for competition nerves.

STUDYING THE TEST

Once you have selected the tests you intend to ride, study them. Identify which figures and movements are required and practise them at home. For example, ride up the centre line in working trot, trot to halt, 20 m working-canter circles, 5 m loops and so on. The photos illustrate the following movements: halt (a); riding corners (b); circles (c); change of rein at trot (d); medium walk (e).

Most competitors ride two tests per horse per day and find their horses go better in their second test. Also, first-test errors can be corrected before riding the second test. However, some riders struggle to memorize two tests per day and they prefer to ride one. If they ride the same test at the next show, and so on, until they know that test well, they will eventually find it easy to ride two tests per competition. Be flexible in order to discover what works best for you.

> **DAVID'S TIP**
>
> Often, a test can be commanded, i.e. be read aloud to you by a reader. It is best to:
> **1.** learn the test whether you intend to follow directions from a commander or not:
> **2.** check the competition rules because, for example, in championships no commanders are allowed.

PRACTISING THE TEST

Ask your trainer to judge you as if you were riding a real test and then identify your weaknesses and strengths. These mock tests help improve your competition potential. If you suffer from competition nerves ask him to put you under controlled pressure.

As much as possible, emulate the stresses you will experience at the show. These practice drills get you ready for the live situation.

After practising, discuss your performance with the trainer. Analyse the good and bad parts and know which areas you should improve before the competition.

Practise until the test runs smoothly. Riding individual movements from a test is different, and easier, than riding through the whole test where the movements can come thick and fast. Check the horse does not anticipate but works from the rider's aids. Do not overpractise; it can kill the freshness of a performance. Be prepared so that competitions run as smooth as silk. Put energy into your competition training and every test will be a good experience.

> **DAVID'S TIP**
>
> Outside influences, such as bright flowers, white boards and unfamiliar noises, can make horses tense and spooky. To avoid your horse becoming distracted, prepare him for new situations that he will meet at competitions. For example, the judge's car will be parked at **C**, so practise riding in an arena with a car parked at **C**.

THE DAY OF THE COMPETITION

The big day has arrived! You have planned it like a military route march and you want to give it your best shot.

WARMING UP

Warm up the horse as you do normally. Ride a few test movements perhaps, but mostly check that the horse is on the aids and in good balance. Do not overtire him, but conserve his energy for the competition.

CHECKING THE ARENA

Go and look at the competition arena. Assess how it will ride, notice the surface material: is it man-made such as sand or rubber, or is it grass? Is your horse familiar with working on such a surface? Is the competition surface the same as the warm-up area? If not, consider how the horse moves while riding outside the arena boards before your test entry. If time allows, watch other horses compete and see how they cope with the surface. This is particularly important when the test arena is grass and where the ground is unlevel and slippery, and also on artificial surfaces that have seen better days. Use your observations to give a professional edge to your test riding.

GETTING READY
TO ENTER THE ARENA

Ride outside the competition boards in a positive manner. Double check that your horse is listening to the aids, fine-tune his gaits and wait for the judge's start signal. Once this is given, you have one minute to enter the arena at the A marker. Think positively and switch into competition gear. Command presence and become irresistible to spectators! Say to yourself, 'I will give my best', and enter the competition arena with panache.

DAVID'S TIP

Attention to detail pays dividends. Give yourself plenty of time to arrive at the show, book into the secretary's office, warm up your horse, ride over to the competition arena, etc.

When competing on grass, fit studs to the horse's shoes; they are a good safety measure and they give the horse extra purchase on the ground. If he slips he could lose confidence and cease to step forwards actively.

RIDING IN A
DRESSAGE COMPETITION

Dressage tests measure the horse's training status according to a recognised standard of dressage. The highest merits are awarded to the best performances of the day. The judge's comments give directions for training and motivate the competitor to improve. They add perspectives of enjoyment.

Focus on the job of riding the test. Go for gold!

ACKNOWLEDGEMENTS

Special thanks to Douglas Hibbert riding Mrs Leslie Darvas' part Trakehner gelding, Hampton, by Paisley Court. Also to Beverly Brightman with her young horse, the bay mare, Brilliance (Hannoverian by Benz) and her grey Hannoverian gelding, Arlequin. The photographs were taken at Addington Equestrian Centre, many thanks for the use of the Centre's facilities.

British Library Cataloguing-in-Publication Data.
A catalogue record for this book is available from the British Library

ISBN 0.85131.807.X

Published in Great Britain in 2001 by
J. A. Allen an imprint of Robert Hale Ltd.,
Clerkenwell House, 45–47 Clerkenwell Green,
London EC1R 0HT

Reprinted 2004

Design and Typesetting by Paul Saunders
Series editor Jane Lake
Colour processing by Tenon & Polert Colour Processing Ltd., Hong Kong
Printed in Malta by Gutenberg Press Ltd.